SCHOLASTIC

Shoe Box Learning Centers

Word Families

by Pamela Chanko

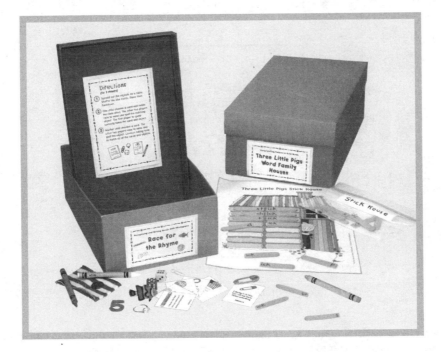

NEW YORK • TORONTO • LONDON • AUCKLAND • SYDNEY
MEXICO CITY • NEW DELHI • HONG KONG • BUENOS AIRES

Teaching *Resources*

For my father, the man of the family,
who gave me my love of words.

Acknowledgments
Grateful thanks to Joan Novelli and Deborah Schecter, excellent
editors and wonderful wordsmiths.

Edited by Joan Novelli
Cover design and photograph by Brian LaRossa
Interior design by Holly Grundon
Interior illustrations by James Graham Hale

ISBN 978-0-545-46870-1

1 2 3 4 5 6 7 8 9 10   40   19 18 17 16 15 14 13 12

CONTENTS

About This Book

Children are naturally drawn to rhyming words and sounds, from nursery rhymes to playground chants. Rhyme makes words fun to play with and easier to remember. Exposing children to word families—words that end in the same sound and spelling pattern—builds on their natural love of rhyme and leads them to become better readers. The more phonograms (the letters in the word family that form the common sound) children learn to recognize, the more words they can read and spell. For example, a child who recognizes the phonogram *-at* can more easily add the words *cat, bat, rat, sat,* and *mat* to his or her sight vocabulary. And once children know what these words look and sound like, the better able they'll be to use them in their own writing. Teaching word families as part of a reading program gives children the tools they need to efficiently decode a wide variety of words, and provides them with the sense of confidence that leads to a lifelong love of reading.

Another important component of any literacy program is independent practice. When children are given the opportunity to use the strategies they've learned (and perhaps discover new ones) on their own, the learning experience takes on a whole new meaning. When children are able to say "I did it all by myself!" they take pride in their own learning and find joy in the process of learning itself. For this reason, the use of independent learning centers as part of a reading and writing program is of paramount importance. Centers not only help children to learn independently but also allow them to practice working in groups—reinforcing the concepts of teamwork, cooperation, and responsibility.

Shoe Box Learning Centers: Word Families allows you to quickly and easily create 30 engaging, portable, hands-on learning centers that teach important literacy skills in fun and creative ways. Making these shoe box learning centers is as easy as photocopying the reproducible labels, directions, and activity pages. Any additional materials that may be needed for a shoe box center, such as crayons, dried beans, or shoelaces, are readily available. The materials for each center fit neatly inside a shoe box, allowing you to stack and store them conveniently and pull them out as needed. With a few shoe boxes and a photocopier, you can create an incredible variety of fun, enriching literacy centers—in a snap!

Setting Up Shoe Box Learning Centers

This book contains 30 shoe box learning centers. The clear organization allows you choose the activities you want to use and set up the shoe box centers quickly and easily. For each center, you'll find:

- **Shoe Box Setup:** For most activities, all you'll need to do is gather the materials and make copies of the reproducible pages. These and any other directions are listed in a "Shoe Box Setup" section for each center.

- **Label and Directions:** A label (shoe box learning center title) and set of student directions is provided for each shoe box learning center. Photocopy these sections of the page onto colored paper (or have children decorate), and cut them out. Glue the label to one end of the shoe box. Glue the student directions to the inside of the box lid.

- **Materials:** An at-a-glance list includes all the items needed for each shoe box learning center. Simply gather the materials and place them in the box.

- **Tips:** These ideas include activity variations and extensions, as well as helpful hints for making the most of children's learning experiences.

- **Reproducible Pages:** Record sheets, story mats, game boards, word cards, mini books, and patterns are just some of the shoe box center supplies included in the book.

Model each shoe box activity for children before having them try it on their own.

A Note on Terminology and Word Family Lists

The teaching of word families centers on phonograms, or the letters in a word family that form the common sound. Phonograms can also be referred to as word endings. (This part of a one-syllable word is also known as a rime.)

The activities in this book were designed to cover the 50 most common word families. However, most of the activities can be expanded or changed to teach any word family, and many of the reproducibles include blank templates for you to plug in your own phonograms.

On page 7 are sample word lists for some of the most common word families, which you can draw from to create your own versions of the shoe box centers. You can also teach different initial consonants, blends, or digraphs by substituting other word beginnings, or onsets.

Reinforcing and Assessing Student Learning

One of the greatest benefits of using centers in the classroom is that they provide teachers with the opportunity to work with small groups or individuals on the concepts and skills being taught. To record students' progress as they move through the shoe box learning centers, you may want to create assessment files. To do so, provide a pocket folder for each student. In the first pocket, place a checklist of all the centers so that students can keep track of those they have completed. (See page 8 for a reproducible Shoe Box Learning Centers Checklist.) In the second, have students store completed record sheets for you to review. For activities that do not require record sheets, sticky notes work well as an assessment tool. Observe students as they work with a shoe box center and ask related questions. Jot comments on sticky notes, and record the child's name, the date, and the shoe box learning center name. Keep these on a separate sheet of paper in the pocket folder for easy reference. In addition, comments for any center can be recorded on the checklist. Use these assessments to guide students' work with the centers. Encourage students to revisit those centers where they show a need for more practice.

Meeting the Common Core State Standards

The center activities in this book will help you meet your specific state language arts standards as well as those recommended by the Common Core State Standards Initiative (CCSSI). The activities support students in meeting standards listed as Foundational Skills for Reading in the CCSSI documents. Students in grades K–2 are expected to demonstrate increasing awareness and competence in the areas that follow. For more details on these standards, go to the CCSSI Web site: www.corestandards.org.

Phonological Awareness
Demonstrate understanding of spoken words, syllables, and sounds (phonemes).

> RF.K.2a, RF.K.2b, RF.K.2c, RF.K.2d, RF.K.2e
> RF.1.2a, RF.1.2b, RF.1.2c, RF.1.2d

Phonics and Word Recognition
Know and apply grade-level phonics and word analysis skills in decoding words.

> RF.K.3a, RF.K.3b, RF.K.3c, RF.K.3d
> RF.1.3a, RF.1.3b, RF.1.3c, RF.1.3d, RF.1.3e, RF.1.3f, RF.1.3g
> RF.2.3a, RF.2.3b, RF.2.3c, RF.2.3d, RF.2.3e, RF.2.3f

To match specific skills and shoe box centers, see the skills matrix on page 9.

Sample Word Family Lists

Short-Vowel Phonograms

Short-*a* Phonograms
- **-ack** back, Jack, pack, quack, rack, sack, black, crack, snack, track
- **-an** ban, can, Dan, fan, man, pan, ran, tan, van, bran, plan, than
- **-ank** bank, sank, rank, tank, yank, blank, clank, crank, drank, thank
- **-ap** cap, gap, lap, map, nap, rap, tap, clap, flap, snap, trap
- **-at** bat, cat, fat, gnat, hat, mat, pat, rat, sat, chat, flat, slat, that

Short-*i* Phonograms
- **-ill** bill, fill, hill, Jill, mill, pill, sill, will, chill, spill, still, thrill
- **-in** bin, fin, pin, tin, win, chin, grin, skin, spin, thin, twin
- **-ip** dip, hip, lip, nip, rip, sip, tip, zip, drip, flip, skip, slip, trip
- **-ing** king, ring, sing, wing, bring, spring, string, swing, thing
- **-ink** link, pink, rink, sink, wink, blink, drink, shrink, think

Short-*e* Phonograms
- **-ell** bell, fell, sell, tell, well, yell, shell, smell, spell
- **-est** best, nest, pest, rest, test, vest, west, zest, chest
- **-et** bet, get, jet, let, met, net, pest, set, wet, yet

Short-*o* Phonograms
- **-ock** dock, knock, lock, rock, sock, tock, block, clock, smock
- **-op** bop, cop, hop, mop, pop, top, chop, drop, flop, shop, stop
- **-ot** cot, dot, got, hot, knot, lot, not, pot, rot, tot, slot, spot

Short-*u* Phonograms
- **-uck** buck, duck, luck, muck, puck, suck, tuck, cluck, stuck, truck
- **-ug** bug, dug, hug, jug, lug, mug, rug, tug, chug, plug, slug, snug
- **-ump** bump, dump, hump, jump, lump, pump, clump, stump, thump

Long-Vowel Phonograms

Long-*a* Phonograms
- **-ail** fail, hail, jail, mail, nail, pail, rail, sail, tail, wail, snail, trail
- **-ake** bake, cake, fake, lake, make, rake, take, wake, shake, snake
- **-ate** date, gate, Kate, late, rate, crate, grate, plate, skate, state
- **-ay** bay, day, hay, lay, may, pay, ray, say, way, clay, play, stay, tray

Long-*i* Phonograms
- **-ice** dice, mice, nice, rice, price, slice, spice, twice
- **-ide** hide, ride, side, tide, wide, bride, glide, pride, slide
- **-ight** fight, knight, light, might, night, right, sight, bright
- **-ine** dine, fine, line, mine, nine, pine, vine, shine, swine

Long-*e* Phonograms
- **-eat** beat, heat, meat, neat, seat, cheat, cleat, treat, wheat
- **-eep** beep, deep, jeep, keep, peep, cheep, sheep, sleep, sweep

Long-*o* Phonograms
- **-oke** joke, poke, woke, broke, choke, smoke, spoke, stroke
- **-old** bold, cold, fold, gold, hold, mold, sold, told, scold

Variant-Vowel Phonograms

- **-air** fair, hair, lair, pair, chair, flair, stair
- **-ar** bar, car, far, jar, tar, scar, star
- **-aw** caw, gnaw, jaw, law, paw, raw, saw, claw, flaw, straw
- **-ore** bore, core, more, sore, tore, wore, chore, score, store

Shoe Box Learning Centers Checklist

Name_____

Shoe Box Learning Center	Date	Comments
My Mini Picture Dictionary		
Egg Scramble Word Builders		
A Wheelbarrow of Words		
Flip-Book Fun		
Squish and Spell		
Elephant Parade		
Word Family House		
Hens and Eggs		
Take the Cake		
Balls in the Air		
Lace Race		
Wally the Word Snake		
Word Family Guessing Game		
Sunken Treasure		
Leaping Lilypads		
Word Family Shape Books		
Race for the Rhyme		
Shake It Up!		
Word Family Print Parade		
Silly Sentence Magnets		
Zoom!		
Word Family Train		
Three Little Pigs Word Family Houses		
Word Family Soup		
Monster Word Builders		
Centipede Slide		
I Spy a Rhyme		
Tower of Rhymes		
Grab Bag Story Starters		
Rebus Rhyme Mini-Books		

Word Family Skills Matrix

Shoe Box Learning Center	Long Vowel	Short Vowel	Long Vowel With Final e	Vowel Digraphs	Other Vowel Sounds	Phonograms Ending in a Single Consonant	Phonograms Ending in Consonant Clusters	Phonograms Ending in Consonant Digraphs	Word Analysis Skills	Word Building Skills
My Mini Picture Dictionary	X	X	X	X	X	X		X	X	X
Egg Scramble Word Builders	X	X	X	X		X	X	X	X	X
A Wheelbarrow of Words	Skills will vary.								X	X
Flip-Book Fun	X	X		X		X	X	X	X	X
Squish and Spell	Skills will vary.								X	X
Elephant Parade	X	X		X		X	X	X	X	
Word Family House	X	X		X		X			X	X
Hens and Eggs	X	X		X		X	X		X	X
Take the Cake	X	X		X		X	X	X	X	
Balls in the Air	Skills will vary.								X	X
Lace Race	X	X	X	X	X	X	X		X	
Wally the Word Snake	X	X	X	X	X	X			X	X
Word Family Guessing Game	X	X				X	X		X	X
Sunken Treasure	X	X	X		X	X	X	X	X	
Leaping Lilypads	Skills will vary.								X	
Word Family Shape Books		X				X		X	X	X
Race for the Rhyme	X	X				X			X	
Shake It Up!	X	X		X		X			X	X
Word Family Print Parade	Skills will vary.								X	X
Silly Sentence Magnets	X	X				X			X	
Zoom!	X			X			X		X	X
Word Family Train	Skills will vary.								X	X
Three Little Pigs Word Family Houses	X	X	X		X			X	X	X
Word Family Soup	X	X	X	X	X	X		X	X	X
Monster Word Builders	X	X		X		X			X	X
Centipede Slide	X	X		X		X	X	X	X	X
I Spy a Rhyme	X	X	X	X	X	X	X	X	X	
Tower of Rhymes	Skills will vary.								X	
Grab Bag Story Starters						X	X		X	
Rebus Rhyme Mini-Books	X	X		X		X			X	X

My Mini Picture Dictionary

Children cut and paste pictures to create their own rhyming dictionaries.

Materials

- shoe box
- box label
- student directions
- scissors
- glue
- mini-book pages (page 11)
- mini-book pictures (page 12)
- resealable plastic bags
- crayons
- pencils

Shoe Box Setup

Copy and cut out the mini-book pages and pictures for each phonogram you'd like to teach. Staple the pages together and write a phonogram on each cover. (Use the following phonograms to go with the pictures on page 12: *-op, -ake, -ail, -ing.*) Place the books, pictures, glue, crayons, and pencils in the shoe box (one book and set of pictures per student; for multiple setups, place materials in resealable bags). Glue the label to one end of the box and the student directions to the inside of the lid.

TIP For a less challenging activity, write the phonogram on each page of the book, leaving a space for children to fill in only the missing initial letters. For a more challenging activity, place all the pictures in the shoe box. Challenge children to find four pictures of things whose names rhyme and to write the words for them.

My Mini Picture Dictionary

Directions

① Choose a mini-book. Write your name on the cover.

② Find the pictures that go in your book. Paste a picture on each page. Write the word on the line.

③ Think of another thing that rhymes. Draw a picture. Write the word on the line.

④ Use your rhyming dictionary to write a silly sentence, poem, or story.

My

Picture
Dictionary

by _____

My Mini Picture Dictionary

Egg Scramble Word Builders

In this game, children scramble word-part eggs to cook up words.

Materials

- shoe box
- box label
- student directions
- scissors
- glue
- egg patterns (page 14)
- score sheet (page 15)
- two clean, empty egg cartons
- dried beans
- pencils

Shoe Box Setup

Make copies of the egg patterns and score sheet. Cut out the eggs. Glue the eggs with word beginnings into each cup of one egg carton. (You can glue them at a slight vertical angle so the eggs look like they are sitting in the carton.) Label the outside of this carton "1." Glue the word-ending eggs inside the second carton. Label this "2." Place a dried bean in each carton and close the lid. Place the cartons, score sheets, and pencils in the shoe box. Glue the label to one end of the box and the student directions to the inside of the lid.

 TIP Make copies of the blank eggs to teach different phonograms. Simply write new word beginnings on one dozen and new phonograms on another dozen.

Building Words With Beginnings and Endings

Egg Scramble Word Builders

Directions

(1) Shake egg carton 1. Open it. Where did the bean land? Write it on the score sheet under Egg 1.

(2) Shake egg carton 2. Open it. Where did the bean land? Write it under Egg 2.

(3) Put the letters together in column 3. If they make a word, give yourself one point. Give yourself an extra point if you can say another word that rhymes.

(4) When the score sheet is full, add up the points. Play again. Can you beat your score?

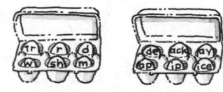

Egg Scramble

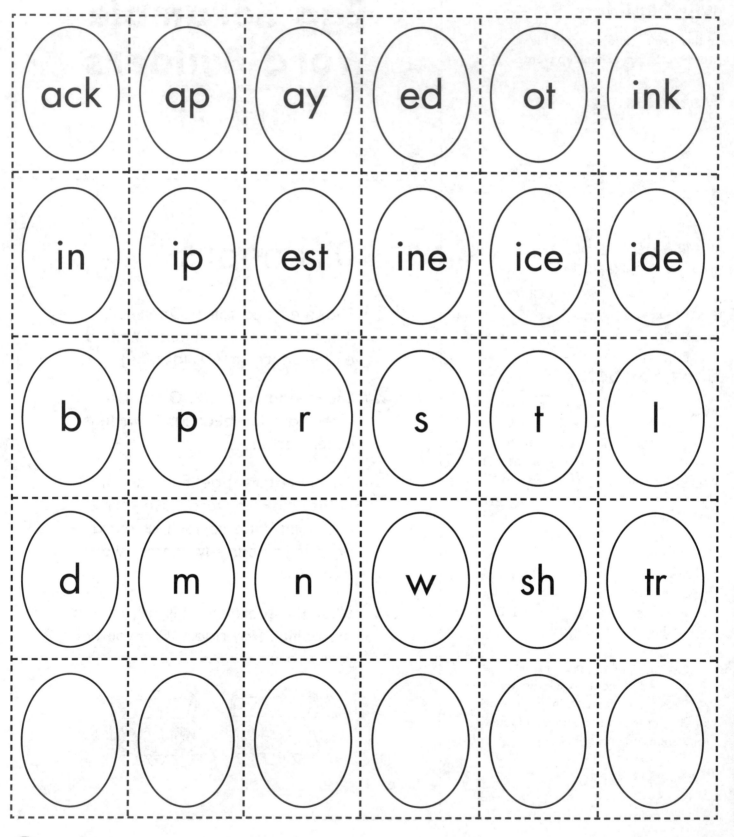

ack	ap	ay	ed	ot	ink
in	ip	est	ine	ice	ide
b	p	r	s	t	l
d	m	n	w	sh	tr

Shoe Box Learning Centers: Word Families © 2012 by Pamela Chanko, Scholastic Teaching Resources

Name _____ Date _____

Egg Scramble Score Sheet

◯ Egg 1	◯ Egg 2	Scramble!	Points

- -

Name _____ Date _____

Egg Scramble Score Sheet

◯ Egg 1	◯ Egg 2	Scramble!	Points

A Wheelbarrow of Words

Children practice reading words with common phonograms in a game that lets them "pick" peas, beans, corn, and more to fill a phonogram wheelbarrow.

Materials

- shoe box
- box label
- student directions
- scissors
- glue
- game board (page 17)
- wheelbarrows and game cards (page 18)
- penny

Shoe Box Setup

Photocopy the game board and laminate. Photocopy the wheelbarrows and cut them out. Write a phonogram on each. Make multiple copies of the game cards. On the back of each, write a consonant, blend, or digraph that will, when combined with a phonogram on a wheelbarrow, make a word. Make at least six cards for each wheelbarrow. Use duplicate consonants, blends, and digraphs if desired. Place the game board, wheelbarrows, game cards, and penny in the shoe box. Glue the label to one end of the box and the student directions to the inside of the lid.

 TIP For record-keeping and assessment, encourage children to list the words they make on paper. Let them read their word lists to you to further reinforce the sound-spelling relationships they're learning.

Building Words With Beginnings and Endings

A Wheelbarrow of Words

Directions
(for 2 or more players)

1. Choose a wheelbarrow. Place the wheelbarrow on Start. Place the game cards in rows picture-side up.

2. Take turns following these directions:

   - Toss a penny. If it lands heads up, move one space. If it lands tails up, move two spaces.

   - Take a card that matches the vegetable on that space.

   - Try to use the letter or letters on the back of the card to make a word with the letters on your wheelbarrow. If you can make a word, keep the card. If not, return the card facedown.

3. Play until each player reaches Finish. Read aloud the words you make.

A Wheelbarrow of Words

A Wheelbarrow of Words

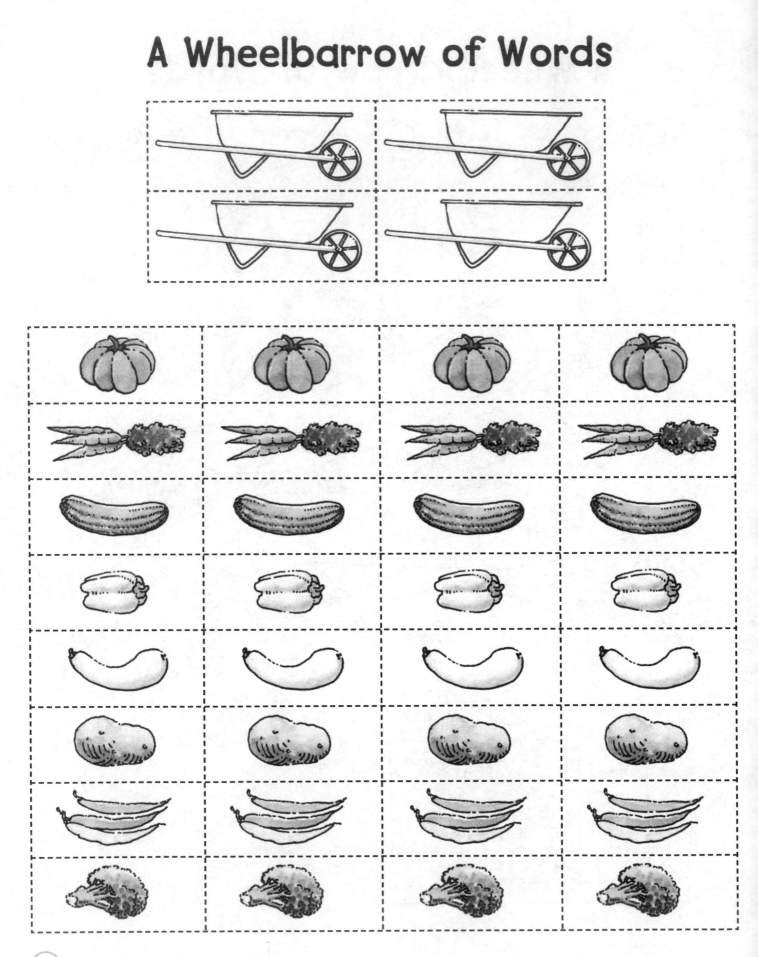

Flip-Book Fun

Children read and illustrate rhyming words with a flip book they create themselves.

Materials

- shoe box
- box label
- student directions
- scissors
- glue
- flip books (pages 20–21)
- hole punch
- paper clips
- paper fasteners
- crayons

Shoe Box Setup

Copy the flip-book pages. Each strip is a set of pages for one flip book (a larger page and two smaller pages). Cut along the dashed lines to make three pages for each book. Punch holes where indicated. Clip each set of flip-book pages together. Place the book pages, paper fasteners, and crayons in the shoe box. Glue the label to one end of the box and the student directions to the inside of the lid.

 TIP Use the blank flip-book strip to create new books for different phonograms. You can also make multiple copies of the small pages (for word beginnings) to expand a single flip book. For an extra challenge, have children attach several of these blank pages to their books and fill in the letters themselves to make new words.

Reading Rhyming Words

Flip-Book Fun

Directions

(1) Take a flip book page. Cut along the dashed lines.

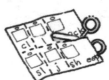

(2) Place the large strip on the bottom. Stack the smaller strips on top. Line up the holes.

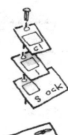

(3) Push a paper fastener through the holes. Bend back the ends.

(4) Flip the pages and read each new word. Draw a picture of each word on the page.

Flip-Book Fun

ock

s

eep

sh

l

j

cl

sl

Flip-Book Fun

ing

r

○

○

s

○

○

k

○

○

Squish and Spell

Children practice letter formation, spelling patterns, and word-building skills using a fun, tactile writing surface.

Materials

- shoe box
- box label
- student directions
- scissors
- glue
- index cards
- markers
- large resealable plastic bags
- clear hair gel
- food coloring
- pencils
- tape

Shoe Box Setup

Write phonograms on index cards (one per card). Fill the resealable bags half full with hair gel. Tint with food coloring. Squeeze the excess air out of the bags and seal. (You may wish to tape the bags closed as well.) Place the phonogram cards, bags, and pencils in the shoe box. Glue the label to one end of the box and the student directions to the inside of the lid.

TIP **F**or more practice, provide record sheets for children to list the words they make for each phonogram card.

Recognizing Spelling Patterns

Squish and Spell

Directions

1 Choose a bag and a card.

2 Place the bag on top of the card. Trace over the letters with your finger or the eraser end of a pencil. Add one or more letters in front to make a word.

3 Squish the bag to erase the letters. Use the same card to make new words.

4 Repeat using different word-ending cards.

Elephant Parade

In this game, children match rhyming words to link elephants from trunk to tail.

Materials

- shoe box
- box label
- student directions
- scissors
- glue
- elephant patterns (page 24)

Shoe Box Setup

On card stock, make four copies of the elephant patterns. Write two words on each elephant: one on the trunk and one on the tail. Use the word sets below to create a starter set of elephants. Place the elephants in the shoe box. Glue the label to one end of the box and the student directions to the inside of the lid.

Sample Word Sets:

cake/bag	rag/shell
bell/top	mop/tail
mail/snake	bake/sell
yell/hop	stop/flag
drag/sail	pail/rake
lake/truck	duck/light
night/sink	drink/nap
cap/luck	pluck/ring
sing/bright	flight/map
tap/rink	link/thing

TIP To make a new game, write words on the elephants that children can link according to features such as initial and final consonant.

Matching Rhyming Words

Elephant Parade

Directions
(for 2 to 4 players)

1. Divide the group of elephants evenly among players. The first player sets out an elephant.

2. The next player reads the word on the elephant's tail. This player looks for an elephant with a word on its trunk that rhymes. The player then links the matching elephants (trunk to tail) to start an elephant parade. If a player does not have a matching elephant, the next player takes a turn.

3. Players continue taking turns adding to the elephant chain until no more matches can be made.

Elephant Parade

Word Family House

Every family needs a home. As children create this special house, they learn about the word family that lives in it.

Materials

- shoe box
- box label
- student directions
- scissors
- glue
- house patterns (page 26)
- pencils

Shoe Box Setup

Copy the house patterns onto sturdy paper and cut them out. You may want to use one color paper for the house and another for the words and pictures. (Precut the windows on the house, if desired.) Place the house patterns, scissors, glue, and pencils in the shoe box. Glue the label to one end of the box and the student directions to the inside of the lid.

TIP Make multiple copies of the house top, and have children make homes for different word families. Simply write the phonogram you'd like children to use on the front door. Have children cut the flaps and glue the pattern to a sheet of plain construction paper. They can lift each flap and paste pictures of and label items belonging to the word family. You might even set aside a special bulletin board for the houses and create a whole word family town!

Using Word-Family Spelling Patterns

Word Family House

Directions

1. Cut along the dashed lines on Part 1 to make window and door flaps for your house. Be sure not to cut on the solid lines.

2. Place Part 1 on top of Part 2. Glue together around the edges. Be sure not to glue down the flaps.

3. Lift the flaps to see what's inside. Write the missing letters.

4. Which word family lives in the house? Write it on the front door. Use the words to tell a story about the family.

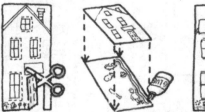

Word Family House

Part 1

Part 2

The

_____

Family

_____ at

_____ at

_____ at

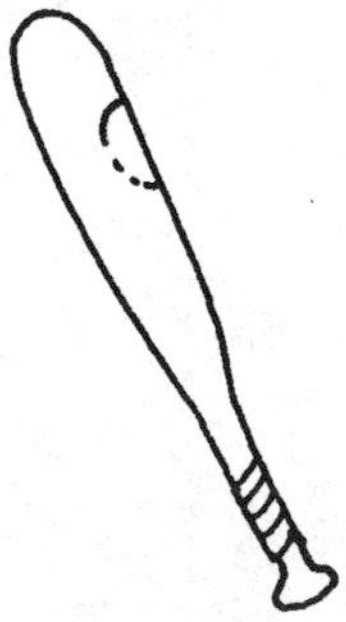

_____ at

_____ at

Hens and Eggs

In a matching game that reinforces word recognition and spelling patterns, children match eggs to their word family hens.

Materials

- shoe box
- box label
- student directions
- scissors
- glue
- henhouse (page 28)
- hens and eggs (page 29)
- resealable plastic bags

Shoe Box Setup

Copy a henhouse and set of hens for each player. Laminate for durability. Copy a set of eggs and cut them out. (Use the blank eggs to add word families.) Place each set of hens in a resealable bag. Place the henhouses, hens, and eggs in the shoe box. Glue the label to one end of the box and the student directions to the inside of the lid.

 TIP For a challenge, include several blank eggs in the set. If children turn over a blank egg, they can say any initial consonant, consonant cluster, or consonant digraph that will make a word when combined with one of their hens. For practice reading different initial consonants, blends, and digraphs, simply white out the word beginnings on the eggs and write new letters to form different words. (Or change the phonograms on the hens and make new eggs as needed.)

Recognizing Spelling Patterns

Hens and Eggs

Directions
(for 2 to 4 players)

 1 Place the eggs facedown. Each player takes a henhouse and a set of hens, and places a hen on each nest.

2 The first player turns over an egg. If it makes a word with the letters on a hen, the player says the word and places the egg on the matching nest. If the egg does not make a word, place it faceup on the table.

3 The next player takes a turn. This player can take an egg that is faceup or choose a new egg.

 4 Play until all the eggs are in a nest or no more matches can be made. Each nest can have more than one egg.

Hens and Eggs

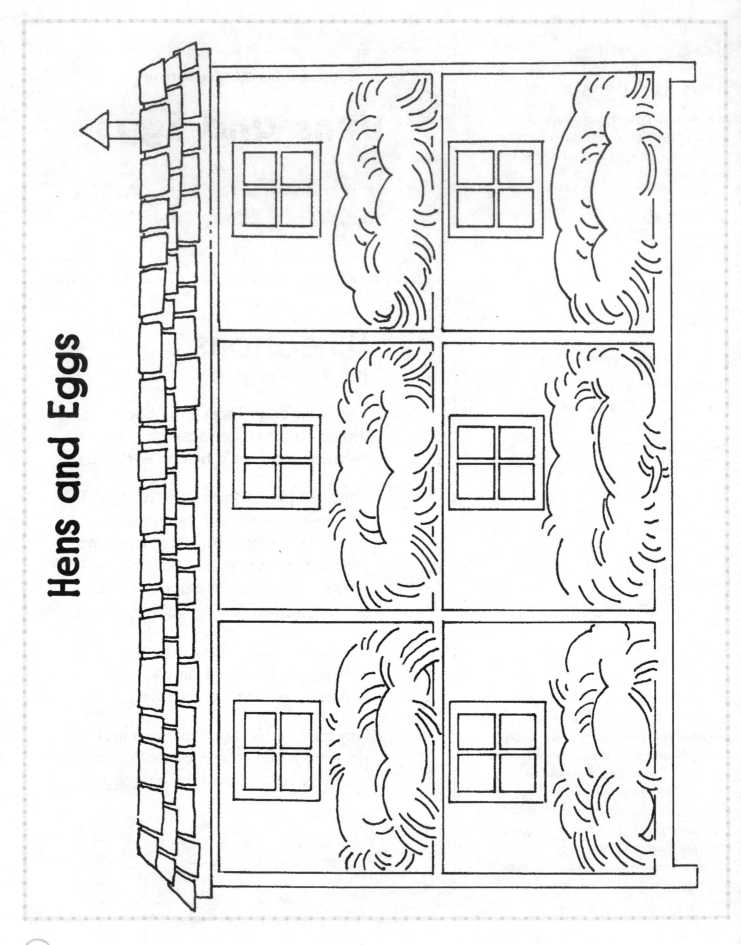

Hens and Eggs

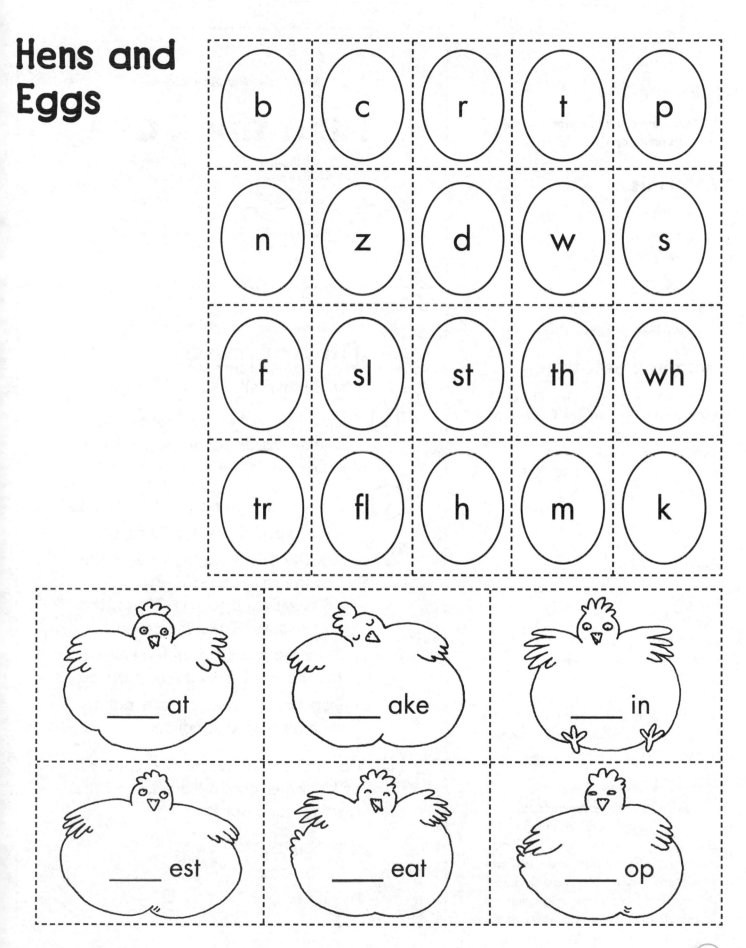

b c r t p

n z d w s

f sl st th wh

tr fl h m k

_____ at

_____ ake

_____ in

_____ est

_____ eat

_____ op

Take the Cake

Children match rhyming words in this variation on a popular card game.

Materials

- shoe box
- box label
- student directions
- scissors
- glue
- cake cards (page 31)

Shoe Box Setup

On card stock make two copies of the cake card patterns. Cut out the cakes, and write one of the following words on each:

slide	ride
sheep	jeep
fill	spill
fine	line
quick	trick
same	game
bee	knee
bright	light
back	track
pay	day
score	more
hot	spot

Place the cards in the shoe box. Glue the label to one end of the box and the student directions to the inside of the lid.

TIP Use the cards to play different games. For example, children might play rhyming rummy or concentration. For a twist on concentration, make two sets of cards and give each player a deck. Children can have a race to see who can match all of his or her cards first.

Matching Rhyming Words

Take the Cake

slide   ride

Directions
(for 2 players)

① Each player takes five cards. Stack the other cards facedown. Turn over one card to make a discard pile.

② Take turns following these directions:
- Read aloud a word on a card.
- Ask the other player if he or she has the rhyming card. If so, he or she gives it to you. If not, this player says "Take the cake!"
- Take the top card on the stack or the top card from the discard pile.
- Display any rhyming word pairs, then discard one card.

③ Play until one player has matched all of his or her cards. Players read their rhyming word pairs.

slide   ride

Take the Cake

Balls in the Air

Children get into the act by sorting juggling balls that belong to the same word family.

Materials

- shoe box
- box label
- student directions
- scissors
- glue
- juggler patterns (page 33)
- milk caps
- permanent marker
- record sheet (page 34)
- pencils

Shoe Box Setup

Copy and cut apart the juggler patterns. Write a word family on each juggler's hat. Laminate the jugglers. Write an initial consonant, consonant cluster, or consonant digraph on each milk cap that, when combined with one of the word families, will make a word. For example, if you write the word families *ack* and *ay* on the jugglers, you could write the letters *cl, p, r, s, t, qu, b, d, m, tr, cl, h,* and *j* on the milk caps. Customize the record sheets to match the word family on each juggler. Place the jugglers, milk caps, record sheets, and pencils in the shoe box. Glue the label to one end of the box and the student directions to the inside of the lid.

TIP For a variation, place each juggler and a set of milk caps in a resealable bag. Use milk caps that will make words as well as one that will not. Have children find out which one doesn't belong.

Balls in the Air

Directions

(1) Choose a juggler. Read the letters on the juggler's hat. Write them on the record sheet.

(2) Choose a milk cap. Add the letter or letters on the milk cap to the letters on the hat. Do they make a word? If they do, place the milk cap above the juggler's hands. If they don't, try a new milk cap.

(3) Add as many milk caps as you can to make words. Complete the record sheet to show the letters you used. Write the letters in the circles. Write the words on the lines.

Balls in the Air

Balls in the Air

Balls in the Air

Name _____

Date _____

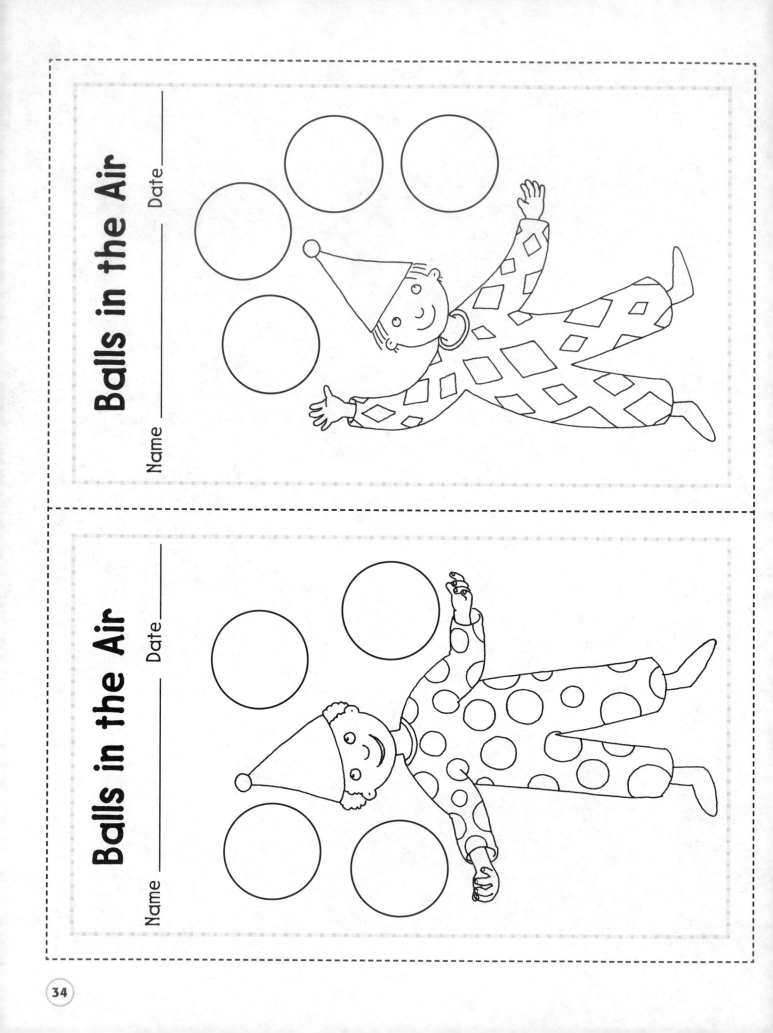

Balls in the Air

Name _____

Date _____

34

Lace Race

Children practice both speed and accuracy as they race to match rhyming words.

Materials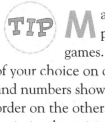

- shoe box
- box label
- student directions
- scissors
- glue
- sneaker patterns (page 36)
- shoelaces
- hole punch

Shoe Box Setup

Copy the sneaker patterns onto card stock. Cut out both sides of each sneaker. Glue the sneaker patterns back-to-back so that they line up. Punch holes where indicated, and laminate if possible. For each sneaker, thread the shoelace through the first hole on the left and tie a knot in back to secure. Place the completed sneakers in the shoe box. Glue the label to one end of the box and the student directions to the inside of the lid.

 TIP **M**ake blank sneaker patterns to create new games. Write rhyming words of your choice on one side of the sneaker and numbers showing the correct lacing order on the other. You can also create a variation by writing initial consonants, blends, or digraphs on the left and word endings on the right. Challenge children to lace up the sneaker to build words.

Matching Rhyming Words

 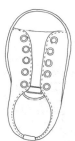

Lace Race

Directions
(for 2 players)

(1) Each player gets a sneaker. One player says "1, 2, 3, Lace!" to begin the game.

(2) Look at the first word on the left. Push the end of the shoelace through the hole next to the rhyming word on the right. Then pull the shoelace back up through the next hole on the left. Again, push the shoelace through the hole next to the rhyming word on the right.

(3) Continue until each player has matched each word with its rhyme.

(4) Turn the sneakers over to check your answers. The player who finishes first wins the race—but only if the words are connected in order!

Lace Race

Lace Race

Wally the Word Snake

In this game, children rely on both word-building skills and chance as they race to reach the finish line.

Materials

- shoe box
- box label
- student directions
- scissors
- glue
- game board (page 38)
- game cards and spinner (page 39)
- game markers (such as different-colored math cubes or tiles)
- paper clip
- paper fastener

Shoe Box Setup

Copy the game board, game cards, and spinner onto card stock. You may wish to laminate them for durability. Cut out the cards and spinner. To create the spinner, push a paper fastener through one end of a paper clip and then through the center of the spinner. Be sure to fasten loosely so the clip will spin easily. Place the board, cards, spinner, and markers in the shoe box. Glue the label to one end of the box and the student directions to the inside of the lid.

TIP For a variation, use correction fluid or tape to change the spaces on the board. Provide word beginnings and a line for word ending. Make cards with word endings.

Practicing Word-Building Skills

Wally the Word Snake

Directions
(for 2 to 4 players)

(1) Place the markers on Start. Stack the cards facedown next to the board.

(2) The first player spins and moves that many spaces on the snake. The player reads the word ending and takes a card. If the letters on the card make a word with the ending on the space, the player stays on the space. If not, the player moves back one space. The next player takes a turn.

(3) After each turn, players return their card to the bottom of the pile. The first player to reach Finish wins the game.

Wally the Word Snake

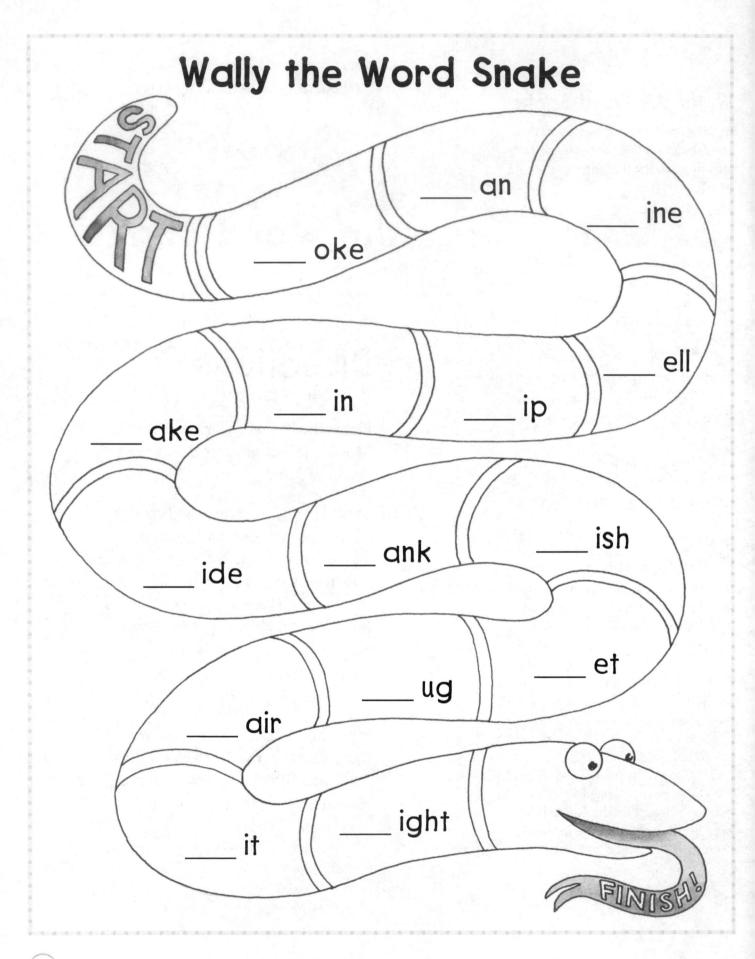

START

____ an

____ ine

____ oke

____ ell

____ in

____ ip

____ ake

____ ish

____ ide

____ ank

____ et

____ ug

____ air

____ ight

____ it

FINISH!

Wally the Word Snake

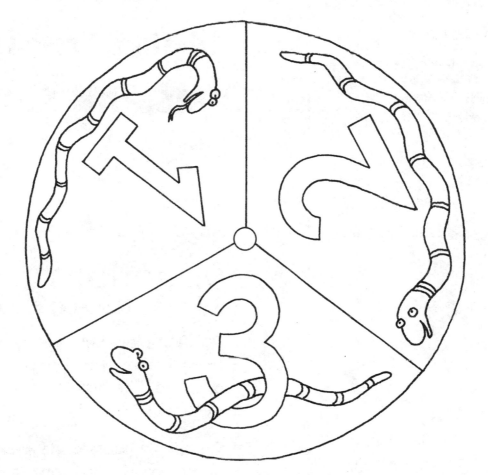

br	f	r	fl
sm	p	ch	m
sn	w	t	j
l	b	sh	s

Word Family Guessing Game

Children play for points in an exciting game that challenges them to guess words in different phonogram categories.

Materials

- shoe box
- box label
- student directions
- scissors
- glue
- game board top (page 41)
- game board bottom (page 42)
- paper
- pencils

Shoe Box Setup

Copy the top and bottom of the game board onto card stock. Cut the top of the board along the dashed lines to make four rows of four flaps each. Be sure not to cut on the solid lines. Staple or glue the game board top to the bottom, attaching the edges so that the flaps do not get glued down. When lined up correctly, the flaps will reveal the answers and points when lifted. Attach a small sticky note to each flap to cover up the clues. Place the game board, paper, and pencils in the shoe box. Glue the label to one end of the box and the student directions to the inside of the lid.

TIP Create a new game by writing in new phonograms at the top of the board. Use additional small sticky notes to write new word clues and answers. Attach the notes to the flaps and to the board's bottom.

Word Family Guessing Game
-ock   -ink   -ack

Directions
(for 2 to 4 players plus "announcer")

 The first player chooses a word family category and points to any clue flap. The announcer uncovers the clue and reads it aloud.

 The player guesses the word and the announcer lifts the flap. If the player was correct, he or she gets the number of points shown.

 Players continue to take turns choosing categories and clue flaps. Each clue can be used only once.

④ When all the clues have been used, players add up their points. The player with the most points wins the game.

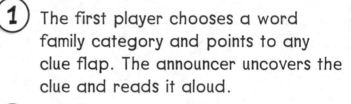

Word Family Guessing Game

_ock	_an	_ink	_ack
It tells time.	It makes a breeze.	You do this when you close you eyes quickly.	Jill went up the hill with him.
It goes on your foot.	You can cook in it.	You can ice skate on it.	You can did this with blocks.
It means someone wants to come in.	You can ride in it.	You wash dishes in it.	It's the opposite of front.
It's another name for a stone.	You can buy soap in it.	This means to get smaller.	A train runs on it.

Word Family Guessing Game

_ock	_an	_ink	_ack
It tells time.	It makes a breeze.	You do this when you close you eyes quickly.	Jill went up the hill with him.
It goes on your foot.	You can cook in it.	You can ice skate on it.	You can do this with blocks.
It means someone wants to come in.	You can ride in it.	You wash dishes in it.	It's the opposite of front.
It's another name for a stone.	You can buy soup in it.	This means to get smaller.	A train runs on it.

Word Family Guessing Game

Jack	blink	clock
100	300	200

stack	rink	sock
400	200	100

back	sink	knock
200	100	400

track	shrink	rock
300	400	300

Sunken Treasure

In this game, children dive for treasure and come up with rhyming words.

Materials

- shoe box
- box label
- student directions
- scissors
- glue
- game board (page 44)
- treasure cards (page 45)
- number cube
- game markers (such as different-colored math cubes or tiles)

Shoe Box Setup

Copy the game board and cards onto card stock, and laminate if desired. Children might like to color the game board and cards first. Cut apart the game cards along the dashed lines. Place the board, cards, number cube, and game markers in the shoe box. Glue the label to one end of the box and the student directions to the inside of the lid.

TIP To incorporate writing and spelling, have children write their rhyming words on a sheet of paper. You might have one child be a "spellchecker." For an even greater challenge, increase the number of rhyming words children must make in order to keep the treasure.

Recognizing Rhyming Words

Sunken Treasure

Directions
(for 2 to 4 players)

(1) Stack the treasure cards facedown in the center of the board. Each player places a marker on a different Start space.

(2) Take turns rolling the number cube. Move that many spaces. Follow any directions on the space.

(3) When a player lands on "Dive!" he or she picks a treasure card and reads the word. If the player can say three more words that rhyme, he or she keeps the card. If not, it is placed on the bottom of the pile.

(4) Continue until all the cards are gone.

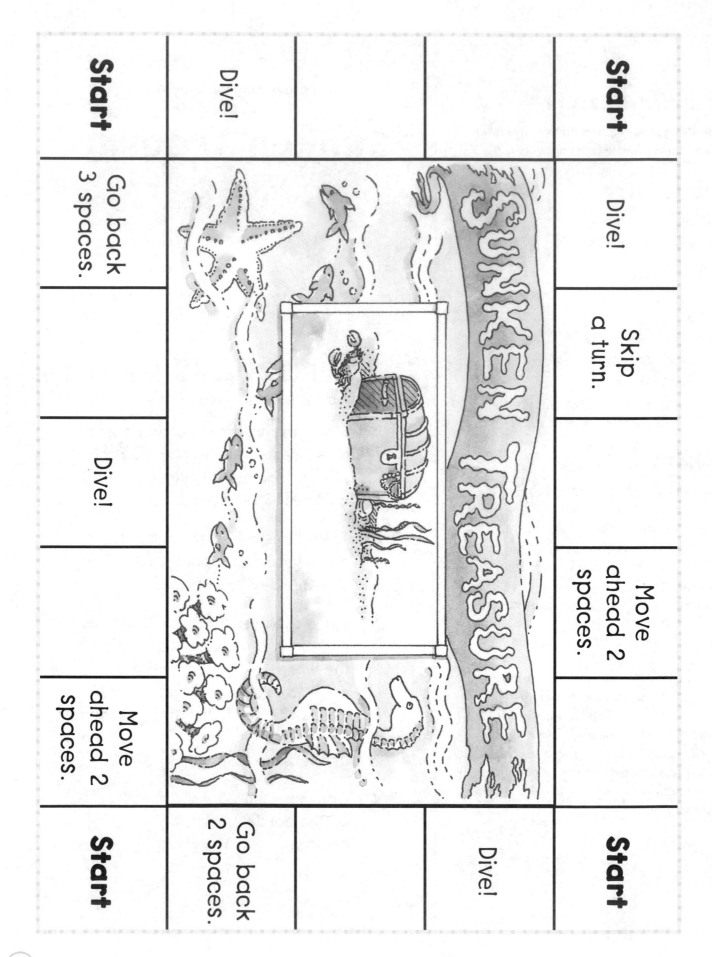

Start

Dive!

Skip a turn.

Move ahead 2 spaces.

Dive!

Start

Go back 3 spaces.

Dive!

Move ahead 2 spaces.

Start

Dive!

Move ahead 2 spaces.

Go back 2 spaces.

Start

SUNKEN TREASURE

Sunken Treasure

ring

shell

crown

bank

gold

lock

chest

sack

map

ship

Leaping Lilypads

Children build word family lists as they hop their frogs from one lilypad to another.

Materials

- shoe box
- box label
- student directions
- scissors
- glue
- game board (page 47)
- frog patterns and record sheet (page 48)
- resealable plastic bags
- number cube
- pencils

Shoe Box Setup

Copy the game board and frogs onto card stock (one set per player). Make copies of the record sheet. For each game board, write six words that represents different phonograms on six random lilypads (one word per lilypad). Write a word that rhymes with each lilypad word on a frog. Place the frogs in a resealable bag. Make a different game board and set of frogs for each player. Place the game boards, frogs, record sheets, number cube, and pencils in the shoe box. Glue the label to one end of the box and the student directions to the inside of the lid.

 TIP For a challenge, invite children to write a new word on each lilypad (on the record sheet) that rhymes with the other two words. Expand the shoe box center by creating new game board and frog sets. Children can help make these, reinforcing spelling patterns in the process.

Leaping Lilypads

Directions
(for 2 or more players)

1. Each player takes a game board, set of frogs, and record sheet. Each player places a frog on Start.

2. Players take turns rolling the number cube and moving their frog. If there is a word on the lilypad, read it. If the word rhymes with the word on the frog, record both words in a lilypad on the record sheet.

3. On each turn players may start a new frog or move a frog already on the board. Players can move a frog around the game board more than once to make a match. The first player to match each frog to a lily-pad wins.

Leaping Lilypads

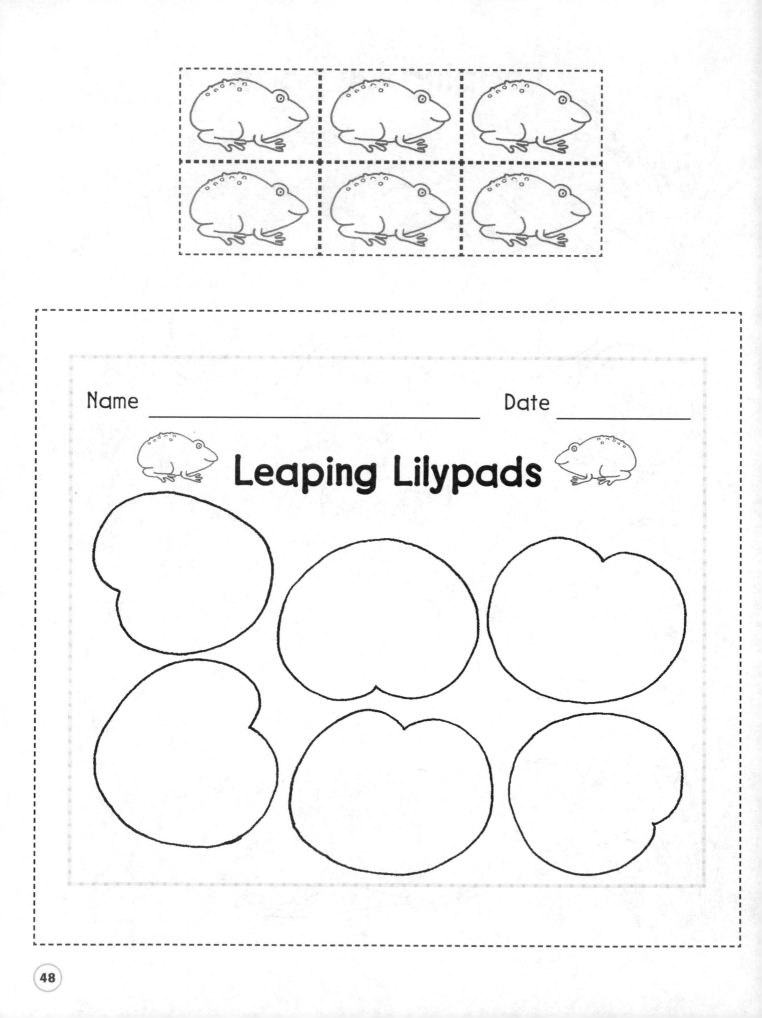

Name _____   Date _____

Leaping Lilypads

Word Family Shape Books

Children use their own pictures and letters to create shape books representing word families.

Materials

- shoe box
- box label
- student directions
- scissors
- glue
- shape book patterns (page 50)
- paper
- pencils
- crayons
- stapler

Shoe Box Setup

Enlarge the shape book patterns and copy onto card stock. Cut out the shapes. Place the patterns, paper, scissors, pencils, crayons, and stapler in the shoe box. Glue the label to one end of the box and the student directions to the inside of the lid.

TIP Refresh this center from time to time with new shape book patterns to reinforce different word families. For example, you might create a ship pattern for the *-ip* family, a baseball cap for the *-ap* family, and a van shape for the *-an* word family.

 # Word Family Shape Books

Directions

1. Choose a shape. What does it look like? Complete the word and write your name to make the book cover.

2. Trace the shape and cut it out to make more pages. On each page, draw a picture of something else in the same word family. Write the word.

3. Staple the pages together to make a book. Read it to a friend.

Word Family Shape Books

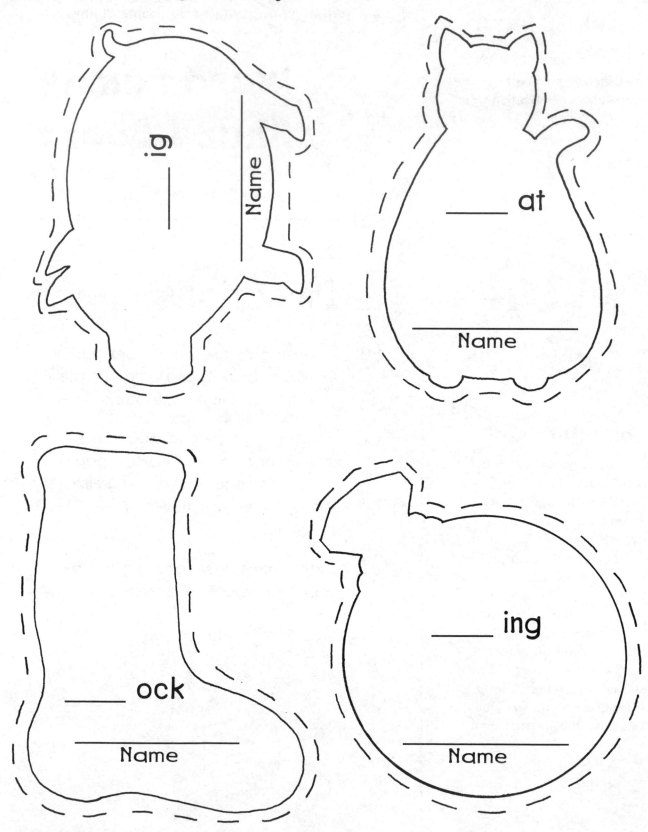

___ig

Name

___ at

Name

___ ock

Name

___ ing

Name

Recognizing and Writing Words With Phonograms

Race for the Rhyme

Children practice spelling patterns as they match objects that have rhyming names.

Materials

- shoe box
- box label
- student directions
- scissors
- glue
- clue cards (page 52)
- resealable plastic bags
- sets of objects (see lists in Shoe Box Setup)

Shoe Box Setup

Copy and cut apart the clue cards. Place each set of cards in a resealable bag and label (short *i*, long *i*). Gather objects to represent each item described in the clue cards, for example:

Short *i*: small stick, toy ring, picture of baseball mitt, picture of a face with arrow pointing to the chin, pink crayon, toy fish, safety pin, paper clip

Long *i*: dice, plastic knife, dime, plastic number 9, piece of striped fabric, white crayon, plastic number 5, picture of an eye

Store each set of objects in a separate bag. Place the clue cards and sets of objects in the shoe box. Glue the label to one end of the box and the student directions to the inside of the lid.

TIP To vary the game, mix up the objects to create sets with combinations of vowel sounds. Rearrange the clue cards accordingly. Make new sets of clue cards and objects to reinforce other phonograms.

Recognizing and Writing Words With Phonograms

Race for the Rhyme

Directions
(for 3 players)

1. Spread out the objects on a table. Shuffle the clue cards. Place them facedown.

2. One child chooses a card and reads the clues aloud. The other two players race to name and spell the matching object. The first player to guess correctly takes the card and object.

3. Another child chooses a card. The other two players race to name and spell the object. Continue taking turns to match up all the cards and objects.

Race for the Rhyme

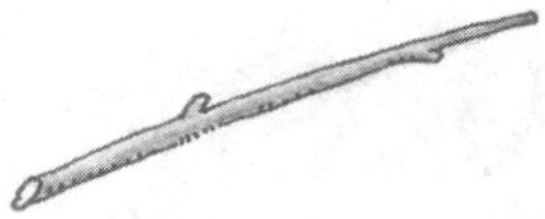

I rhyme with *brick*. You can find me near a tree.

(short *i*)

I rhyme with *sing*. You can wear me on a finger.

(short *i*)

I rhyme with *sit*. You can catch a ball with me.

(short *i*)

I rhyme with *win*. You can find me on a face.

(short *i*)

I rhyme with *link*. You can make me by mixing red and white.

(short *i*)

I rhyme with *swish*. You can find me swimming in a school.

(short *i*)

I rhyme with *win*. You can use me to fasten something.

(short *i*)

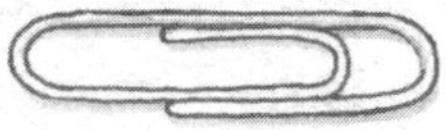

I rhyme with *tip*. You can use me to hold papers together.

(short *i*)

We rhyme with *mice*. You can roll us in a game.

(long *i*)

I rhyme with *life*. You can use me to cut a sandwich.

(long *i*)

I rhyme with *lime*. You can use me to buy something.

(long *i*)

I rhyme with *mine*. You can find me before 10.

(long *i*)

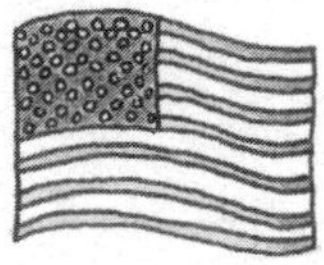

I rhyme with *ripe*. You can see me on the American flag.

(long *i*)

I rhyme with *bite*. You can mix me with red to make pink.

(long *i*)

I rhyme with *hive*. You can use me to count quickly.

(long *i*)

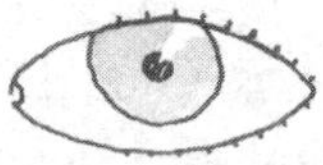

I rhyme with *bye*. You can find me on a face.

(long *i*)

Shake It Up!

In this game, children learn to recognize spelling patterns as they build words in common families.

Materials

- shoe box
- box label
- student directions
- scissors
- glue
- cube patterns (page 54)
- plastic or paper cup
- paper
- pencils

Shoe Box Setup

Copy the cube patterns onto sturdy paper and cut them out. Follow the directions for folding and gluing. Place the cubes, cup, paper, and pencils in the shoe box. Glue the label to one end of the box and the student directions to the inside of the lid.

TIP Use the blank cube template to reinforce different spelling patterns. Make four copies. Write phonograms on two of the cubes and initial consonants, clusters, or digraphs on the other two cubes.

Using Spelling Patterns to Spell Words

Shake It Up!

  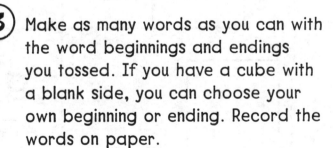

Directions
(for 2 to 4 players)

1. Place the cubes in the cup.

2. Take turns shaking the cup and tossing the cubes on the table.

3. Make as many words as you can with the word beginnings and endings you tossed. If you have a cube with a blank side, you can choose your own beginning or ending. Record the words on paper.

Cube Patterns

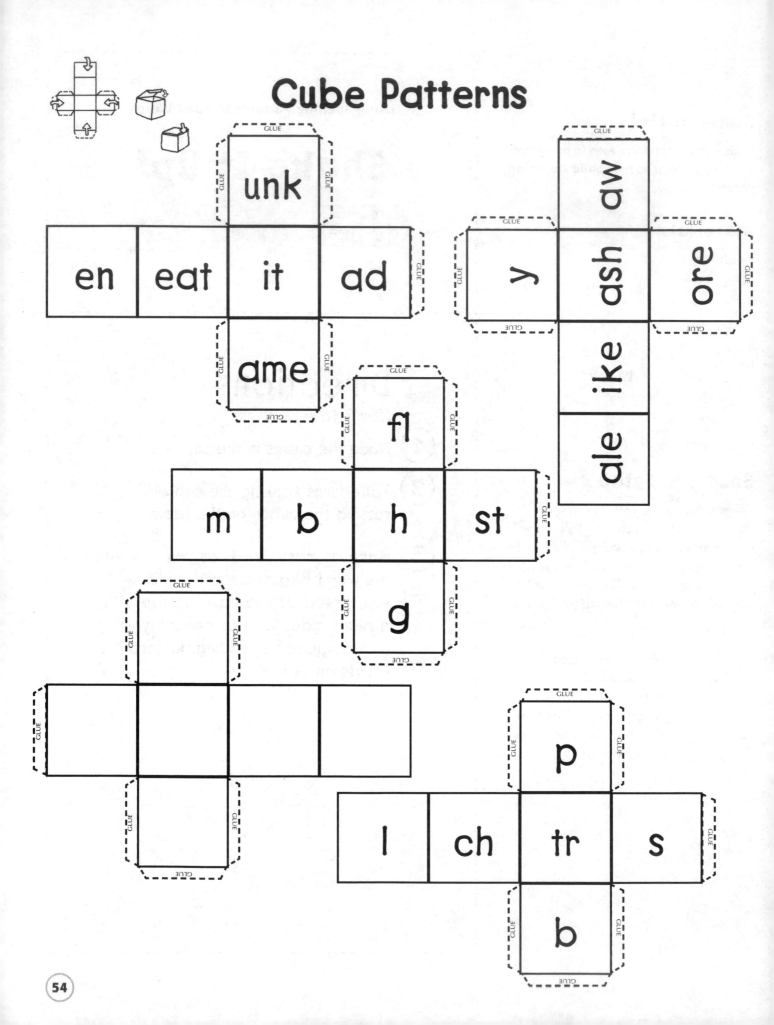

unk

en | eat | it | ad

ame

aw

y | ash | ore

ike

ale

fl

m | b | h | st

g

l | ch | tr | s

p

b

Word Family Print Parade

Children learn to recognize spelling patterns in environmental print as they go on a scavenger hunt through newspapers and magazines.

Materials

- shoe box
- box label
- student directions
- scissors
- glue
- newspapers, magazines, and flyers

Shoe Box Setup

Gather newspapers, magazines, flyers, and advertisements. Large-print periodicals (such as those geared toward children or seniors) work especially well. Create a record sheet by dividing a sheet of paper into several columns and labeling each with a word family. Make multiple copies. Set aside an eye-level wall space for a "Word Family Print Parade" on which children can display their completed work. Label a separate section on the wall for each word family. Place print materials, record sheets, scissors, and glue in the shoe box. Glue the label to one end of the box and the student directions to the inside of the lid.

 TIP Extend the activity by having children hunt for different phonograms. Simply white out the phonograms on the sheet and write new ones in the boxes.

Recognizing Spelling Patterns

Word Family Print Parade

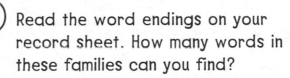
sale   best   yum

Directions

1. Read the word endings on your record sheet. How many words in these families can you find?

2. Look through the newspapers and magazines. Each time you find a word, cut it out and paste it in the box.

3. Fill each box with as many words as you can.

4. Cut apart the boxes. Display your work in the Word Family Print Parade.

-ale	-est	-op	-ide
SALE	Best	SHOP	guide

Silly Sentence Magnets

In this variation on the popular "magnetic poetry" pastime, children sort words into families and use them to create silly sentences.

Materials

- shoe box
- box label
- student directions
- scissors
- glue
- word magnet cards (page 57)
- self-stick magnetic tape
- small magnetic boards
- resealable plastic bags

Shoe Box Setup

Copy the word magnet cards onto card stock. You may wish to make several copies of the sentence-builder cards, as these words will probably be used multiple times. Laminate the cards for durability. To create the magnets, cut out each strip of words and attach a piece of magnetic tape to the back. Cut apart the words in each strip. Place the word family magnets in a bag and label it. Place the sentence-builder magnets in a bag and label it. Place the magnets and magnetic boards in the shoe box. Glue the label to one end of the box and the student directions to the inside of the lid.

 To reinforce sentence format, make magnets for words such as *The*, *I*, *A*, and *An*, using initial capital letters. Expand this center by making additional word family and sentence-builder word magnets.

Building Sentences With Rhyming Words
Silly Sentence Magnets

Directions

(1) Sort the word family magnets into piles. Make one pile for each word family.

(2) Choose a word family pile and place the magnets on the board.

(3) Add the sentence-builder magnets to the board. Move the magnets around to make a silly sentence. Read the sentence to a friend.

(4) Repeat, using new word family magnets.

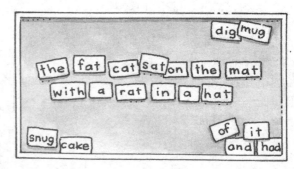

Silly Sentence Magnets

Word Family Magnets

hat	fat	lake	pig	big
mat	rat	shake	jig	twig
sat	snake	fake	wig	bug
cat	cake	bake	dig	snug
hug	mug	nice	mice	rug

Sentence-Builder Magnets

the	have	I	is	and
was	went	did	saw	are
on	in	that	a	of
to	or	with	were	it
they	had	.	!	?

Zoom!

Children build words and learn about long-vowel sounds and spelling patterns as they zoom cars around city streets.

Materials

- shoe box
- box label
- student directions
- scissors
- glue
- street map (page 59)
- removable stickers
- small toy cars
- paper
- pencils

Shoe Box Setup

Enlarge the street map on card stock. You may wish to laminate it for durability. Use removable stickers to label the cars with the following phonograms: *-ate, -ake, -eat, -old, -eep, -ine, -eet, -ice.* Place the map, cars, paper, and pencils in the shoe box. Glue the label to one end of the box and the student directions to the inside of the lid.

TIP For a new game, change the stickers to focus on short-vowel phonograms such as *-in, -ed, -up, -ot, -at, -ack,* and *-ick.* If necessary, white out the letters on the street signs to add new letters that will easily form words when added to the beginning of the new phonograms.

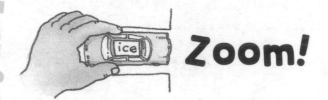

Practicing Long-Vowel Sounds and Spelling Patterns

Zoom!

Directions

(1) Look at the street map. Read the street signs. The street names are word beginnings.

(2) Look at the cars. The letters on the cars are word endings.

(3) Choose a car. Put your car on Start. Now drive! For each street you come to, try to make a word. If the street sign letter and your car letters make a word, write it on a sheet of paper. Drive to as many streets as you can. Make as many words as you can.

(4) Choose a new car. Make new words.

Zoom!

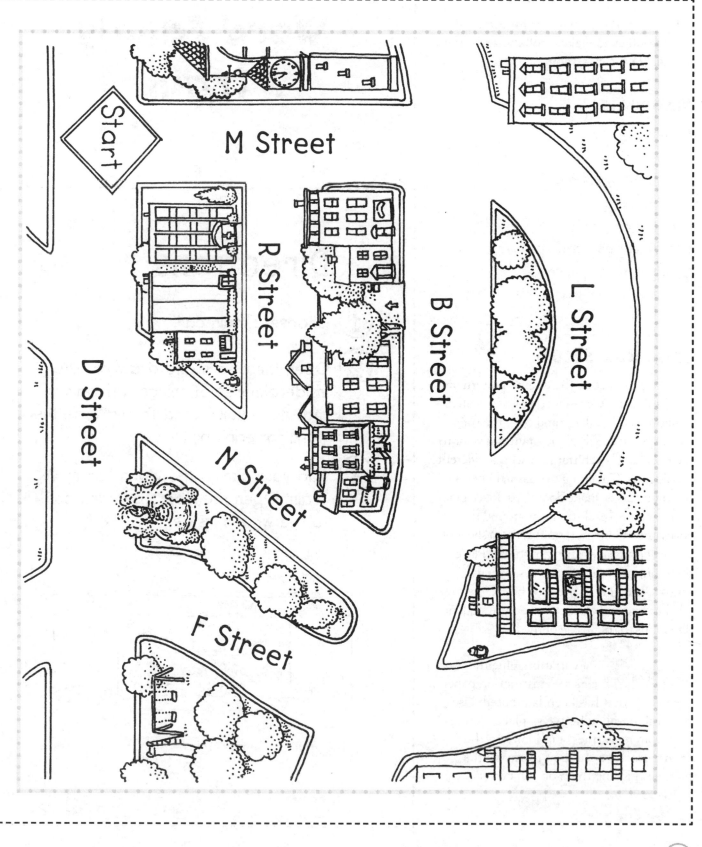

Start

M Street

R Street

B Street

L Street

D Street

N Street

F Street

Word Family Train

Children create special cars for different word families to make a collaborative train banner for the classroom.

Materials

- shoe box
- box label
- student directions
- scissors
- glue
- train car patterns (page 61)
- construction paper
- pictures from magazines
- pencils

Shoe Box Setup

Enlarge and copy the engine pattern and display in an eye-level spot on a wall or bulletin board. Enlarge and copy the train car pattern for each phonogram you want to include. Label each train car with a different phonogram. Cut along the dashed lines on the train cars to make door flaps. Place glue on the back of each train car around the edges only. Glue each train car to a sheet of construction paper and trim to size. Place the train car patterns, pictures, pencils, scissors, and glue in the shoe box. Glue the label to one end of the box and the student directions to the inside of the lid.

 TIP As a variation, glue the train cars to construction paper that has been laminated. Use removable wall adhesive to place pictures (cut from magazines) randomly on the train cars. Have children rearrange the pictures, placing them on the correct train cars.

Word Family Train

Directions

(1) Choose a train car.

(2) Open the doors and draw or glue inside pictures of things with names that go in your word family. Write the word for each picture.

(3) Add your car to the Word Family Train. Open the doors on each car to see what's inside!

Word Family Train

All Aboard the Word Family Train!

_____ Car

Three Little Pigs Word Family Houses

In this fun fairy tale game, children build word-family houses for the three little pigs to keep out the big, bad wolf!

Materials

- shoe box
- box label
- student directions
- scissors
- glue
- house patterns (pages 63–65)
- 10 craft sticks, cut in half
- 20 stones (each about an inch long)
- yellow tagboard (20 ½- by 2-inch pieces)
- 3 resealable plastic bags

Shoe Box Setup

Copy and laminate the houses. Write *ick* on eight craft stick halves (near the left edge). On the remaining halves, write *st, br, ch, k, cl, p, t, tr,* and the distractors *z, g, v,* and *c* (near the right edge). Write *one* on eight stones. On the remaining stones, write *st, b, c, ph, t, z, sh, thr,* and the distractors *tr, f, j,* and *r.* Write *aw* on eight pieces of tagboard straw. On the remaining pieces, write *str, cl, j, fl, p, r, s, dr,* and the distractors *b, d, t,* and *tr.* Place each set of materials (sticks, stones, and straw) in a bag. Place the houses and bags in the shoe box. Glue the label to one end of the box and the student directions to the inside of the lid.

TIP To reinforce more spelling patterns, write new phonograms and initial consonants on sticks, stones, and straw.

Using Spello Build Words

Three Little Pigs Word Family Houses

Directions

① Choose one of the three little pigs' houses. Take a matching bag of building materials.

② Build the pigs' house by matching word beginnings with word endings. To make a word, place one of each in spaces that are side by side. (You will have some word beginnings left over.)

③ Build words until your house is complete.

Three Little Pigs Stick House

Three Little Pigs Stone House

Three Little Pigs Straw House

Word Family Soup

Children stir up a bowl of alphabet soup with this recipe for word-building fun.

Materials

- shoe box
- box label
- student directions
- scissors
- glue
- soup bowl patterns (page 67)
- short rigatoni noodles
- permanent marker
- small covered pot
- ladle
- pencils

Shoe Box Setup

Make copies of the soup bowl pattern page. Cut apart the soup bowls. Laminate several. Use the others for record sheets. On pasta, write the following phonograms, initial consonants, consonant clusters, and consonant digraphs (one per noodle): *ank, ook, oat, ose, all, un, ish, own, op, ar, ack, eat, ing, aw, ape, unk, ay, ed, ink, ate, ad, ice, it, id, b, c, n, t, d, f, s, r, l, p, k, m, w, g, h, j, cr, ch, st, fl, sh, dr, tr, pl.* Place all noodles in the pot and cover. Place the soup bowls, record sheets, noodle pot, ladle, and pencils in the shoe box. Glue the label to one end of the box and the student directions to the inside of the lid.

TIP To expand the center, write new phonograms on noodles and make duplicate sets of the word-beginning noodles. Add the new noodles to the pot.

Building Words With Recognizable Chunks

Word Family Soup

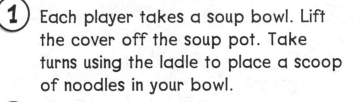

Directions

(for 2 or more players)

(1) Each player takes a soup bowl. Lift the cover off the soup pot. Take turns using the ladle to place a scoop of noodles in your bowl.

(2) Move the noodles around to make as many words as you can without reusing  any noodles. Record the words you make on a soup bowl record sheet.

(3) When you have made all the words you can, compare bowls. How many different words did you make together? How many of those words are three letters? Four? Five?

(4) Return your noodles to the pot. Give the noodles a stir, then play again.

Name _____ Date _____

Word Family Soup

Name _____ Date _____

Word Family Soup

Monster Word Builders

Children build words with the same phonogram to make a monster.

Materials

- shoe box
- box label
- student directions
- scissors
- glue
- monster patterns (page 69)
- paper
- markers or crayons

Shoe Box Setup

Make multiple copies of the monster patterns. Cut out each shape along the dashed lines. Place the monster shapes, glue, and markers or crayons in the shoe box. Glue the label to one end of the box and the student directions to the inside of the lid.

TIP To expand the activity, use correction fluid to change the letters on a copy of the monster patterns. Add copies of the new patterns to the shoe box. For a lively display, invite children to combine their creatures on a word-builders bulletin board, adding details to create a monstrous scene.

Forming Words With Phonograms

Monster Word Builders

Directions

① Choose a monster body. Say the sound the letters make. Glue the monster body to a sheet of paper.

② Find heads, arms, legs, and tails that make words with those letters. Glue each part to the body to build a monster.

Monster Word Builders

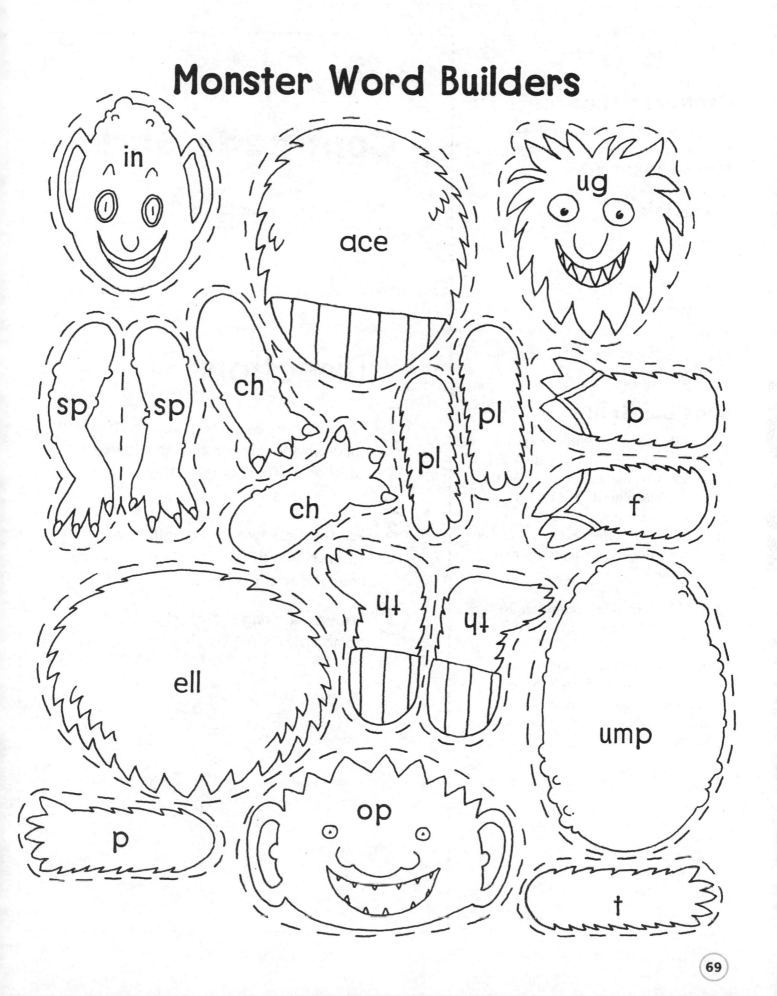

Centipede Slide

Children practice building words and finding rhymes with a slide-through game they create themselves.

Materials

- shoe box
- box label
- student directions
- scissors
- glue
- centipede pattern and word strips (page 71)

Shoe Box Setup

Copy the centipede pattern and word strips onto card stock. Cut slits on the centipede along the dashed lines. Cut the strips apart along the dashed lines. Place the strips and the centipede pattern inside the shoe box. Glue the label to one end of the box and the student directions to the inside of the lid.

TIP Use multiple copies of the blank strip to teach different word beginnings and endings. Write initial consonants, consonant clusters, or consonant digraphs on one strip, phonograms on the next, and an additional rhyming word from each family on the last.

Building Rhyming Words

Centipede Slide

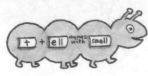

Directions

1. Thread the "Beginning" letter strip through the slits on the first circle as shown. Thread the other strips through the slits as shown.

2. Pull the first two strips until you make a word. Pull the third strip until you find a rhyme.

3. Repeat, making different combinations of words and rhymes.

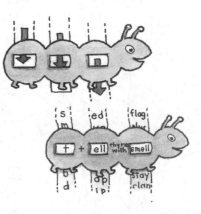

Centipede Slide

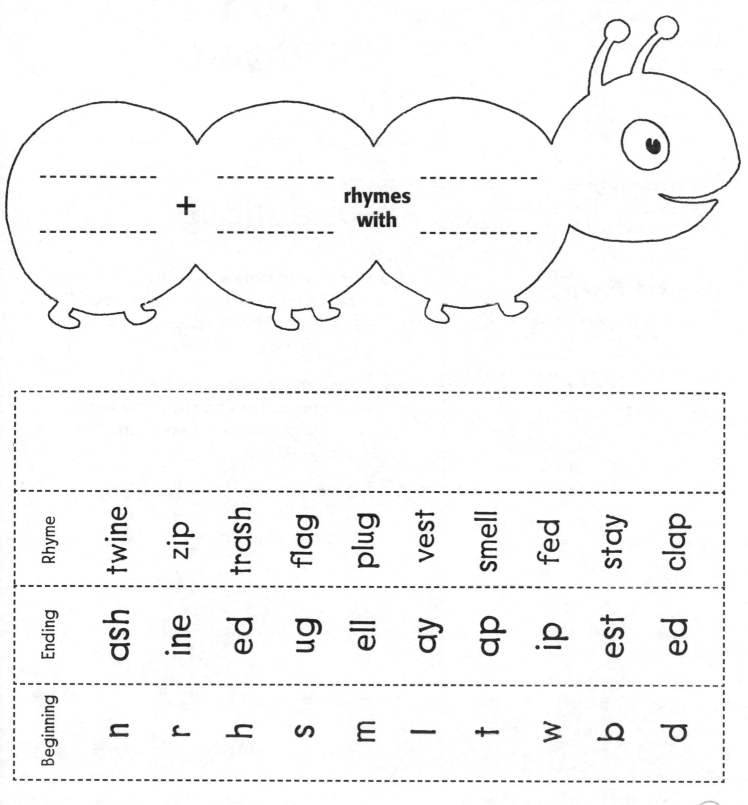

+   rhymes with

Rhyme	twine	zip	trash	flag	plug	vest	smell	fed	stay	clap
Ending	ash	ine	ed	ug	ell	ay	ap	ip	est	ed
Beginning	n	r	h	s	m	l	t	w	b	p

I Spy a Rhyme

In this version of I Spy, children find rhyming objects around the classroom.

Materials

- shoe box
- box label
- student directions
- scissors
- glue
- game board (page 73)
- game markers (such as different-colored math cubes or tiles)
- penny

Shoe Box Setup

Copy the game board onto card stock and laminate if you wish. Place the game board, markers, and penny in the shoe box. Glue the label to one end of the box and the student directions to the inside of the lid.

TIP Make additional versions of this game by using correction fluid or tape to change the words. To incorporate writing, provide paper and pencils so children can keep a record of rhyming word pairs.

Recognizing Word Patterns

I Spy a Rhyme

Directions
(for 2 players)

 Place your markers on Start. The first player tosses a penny. If it lands heads up, move 1 space. If it lands tails up, move 2 spaces.

 Look at the picture and the word on the space. Then point to something in the classroom that rhymes. Say "I spy a [rhyming word]."

 Continue taking turns and spying rhymes. The first player to reach Finish wins the game.

I Spy a Rhyme

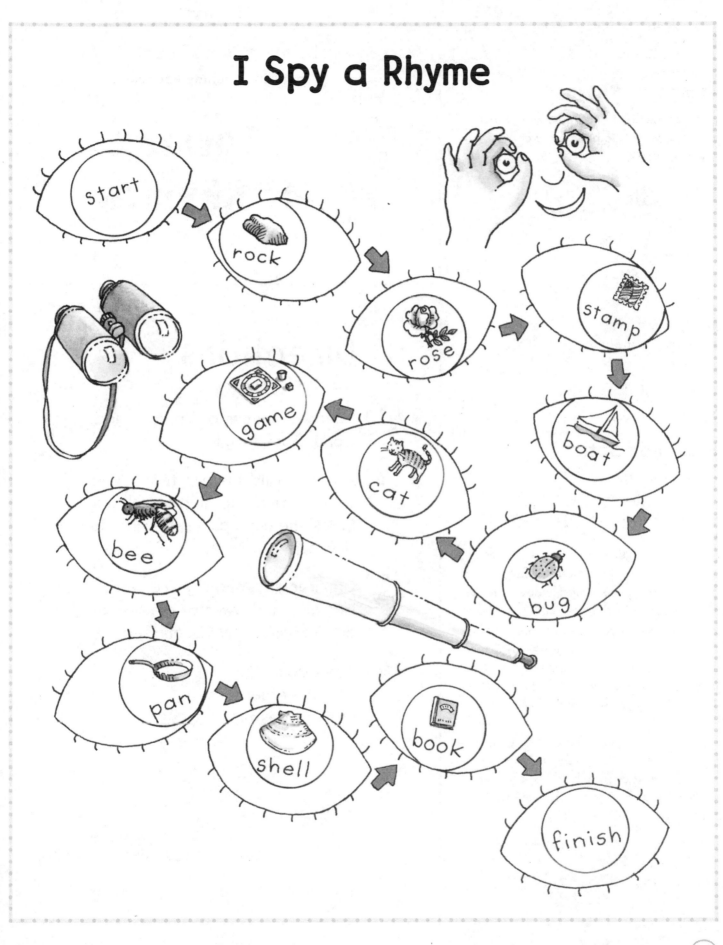

Tower of Rhymes

Children match phonograms with short and long vowels to build a tower of rhyming words.

Materials

- shoe box
- box label
- student directions
- scissors
- glue
- small paper cups
- marker
- paper
- pencils

Shoe Box Setup

Generate a list of rhyming word pairs, with each pair belonging to the same word family. (See page 7 for sample words.) Write each word two times on a small cup—once right side up, then again upside down (so that whether the cup is placed right side up or upside down on the tower, the word will be readable). Make at least 20 sets of rhyming word cups. Mix up the cups and place them, along with paper and pencils, in the shoe box. Glue the label to one end of the box and the student directions to the inside of the lid.

TIP To incorporate writing, have children keep a list of words as they go. Challenge children to try to beat their record the next time they play.

Recognizing Spelling Patterns

Tower of Rhymes

Directions
(for 2 players)

1 Player 1: Choose a cup and read the word. Place it right side up.

2 Player 2: Find the cup that rhymes with the first cup. Read both words. Stack the cup upside down on the first cup.

3 Continue stacking rhyming words. Play until the tower of rhymes topples or all rhymes have been used.

4 Play again. This time the other player goes first.

Grab Bag Story Starters

With these surprise sets of words, children use their creativity as they learn word families.

Materials

- shoe box
- box label
- student directions
- scissors
- glue
- grab bag word cards (page 76)
- tagboard
- brightly-colored paper bags
- paper
- pencils
- crayons

Shoe Box Setup

Copy the grab bag cards. Cut them out (use scissors with a decorative edge for a playful touch), and frame each on a slightly larger sheet of colorful tagboard. Place each set of cards in a bag labeled "Grab Bag Story Starters." Place the bags, paper, pencils, and crayons in the shoe box. Glue the label to one end of the box and the student directions to the inside of the lid.

TIP You may want to set aside a bulletin board or wall space in your classroom to display children's stories and pictures. You can follow the format to create new sets of grab bag cards. (See page 7 for word lists.) Use a different-colored marker for each set of words to assist students in returning the words to the correct bags when they're finished.

Writing Words With Recognizable Chunks

Grab Bag Story Starters

Directions

(1) Choose a grab bag. Without looking, take four cards from the bag.

(2) Use the words to tell a silly story.

(3) Draw a picture of your story.

A frog on a log saw a dog in the fog.

Grab Bag Story Starters

Set 1	Set 2	Set 3	Set 4	Set 5
Stan	fat	frog	bug	trip
can	cat	jog	jug	slip
fan	mat	log	rug	zip
man	rat	bog	hug	tip
Jan	hat	fog	slug	flip
pan	bat	hog	tug	rip
plan	splat	smog	snug	skip
ran	flat	dog	dug	blip

Rebus Rhyme Mini-Books

In this interactive mini-book, children use pictures and words to create rebus rhymes.

Materials

- shoe box
- box label
- student directions
- scissors
- glue
- mini-book pages and rebus cards (page 78)
- stapler
- resealable plastic bags
- crayons
- pencils

Shoe Box Setup

Enlarge and copy the mini-book pages and rebus cards. Cut apart the book pages, add a cover, and staple them together in order. Cut out the rebus cards. Store each book and set of cards in a separate resealable bag to make a kit. Place the book kits, crayons, pencils, and glue in the shoe box. Glue the label to one end of the box and the student directions to the inside of the lid.

TIP As a variation, write each line of the rebus rhymes on a sentence strip. Enlarge the pictures, glue to sentence strips, and trim to size. Write the words for those pictures on sentence strips and trim to size. Provide students with sentence strips, picture cards, and word cards. Let them match up pictures and words to complete each rhyme.

Recognizing Spelling Patterns in Connected Text

Rebus Rhyme Mini-Books

Directions

1. Write your name on the cover of the book. Read each page.

2. Find the pictures that will make each poem rhyme. Paste them in the boxes where they make sense.

3. On the last page, draw pictures in the boxes to go with the words. Write a word that will complete the rhyme.

4. Read your book to a friend.

Rebus Rhyme Mini-Books

2

There once was a ☐

who ate lots of ☐ .

When he was done,

he swam in the lake.

4

cat ☐

rat ☐

There once was a ☐

who was friends with a ☐

They liked to play games with a ☐

ball and a _____ .

1

There once was a ☐

who rode in a ☐ .

When she got tired,

she went to sleep.

3

There once were some ☐

who liked to eat ☐ .

They liked it so much,

they did it twice.

jeep | rice | cake | sheep | mice | snake

More Easy-to-Make Shoe Box Learning Centers

Add to your supply of shoe box learning centers periodically by creating fresh activities to keep student interest strong. Following are more ideas for making shoe box centers that reinforce counting skills. For each, use the reproducible templates (right) to make a label and write student directions. Glue the label to the outside of the box and the student directions to the inside of the lid.

Word Family Forest

In this twist on a "family tree," children sort words to see how they are related.

Make and laminate at least four tree patterns. Make and cut out a dozen or so leaf shapes for each tree. Write a word on each leaf to create sets of words that have a phonogram in common. Place all the leaves in a resealable plastic bag. Place the trees and leaves in the shoe box. Have children sort the words onto the trees by word families, reading each set of words when they are finished.

Directions

Penny Word Toss

Children build words in a game that combines skill, chance, and knowledge of spelling patterns.

Make a game board by drawing a 4 by 4 grid on a sheet of paper. Write a combination of phonograms, consonants, consonant clusters, and consonant digraphs on the squares (one per square). Choose a combination that will allow children to build words.

Place the game board, along with two pennies, in the shoe box. To play, have children follow these steps:

- The first player flicks a penny onto the board. This child then looks for another square that will make a word when the letters of both squares are put together. The child flicks a second penny, aiming for that square. If the penny lands on that space, the player reads the word and scores two points. If the penny lands on a different square that makes a word, the score is one point.

- Players take turns flicking the pennies and making words. Play until one player reaches ten points (or any other chosen number). Or play until each player has taken five or another number of turns. Players can then add up their points and try to beat their own scores on a second round.

Tic-Tac-Rhyme!

In this version of tic-tac-toe, players use word families as their X's and O's!

Make word cards for phonograms you want to reinforce. Include at least five cards for each phonogram. Place each set of cards in a resealable plastic bag and label by phonogram. Make and laminate a tic-tac-toe board with spaces sized to fit the word cards. Place the word cards and game board in the shoe box. To play, have children take turns putting cards on spaces. Each player tries to make a line of

rhymes—across, down, or diagonally. Each player also tries to block the other from making a line. If a player makes a line of rhymes, he or she calls "Tic-Tac-Rhyme!" and wins the game. Children can choose different word families and play again.

Rhyme Time

In this game, children race to build words from different families and then look for rhyming words.

Make a set of game cards by writing phonograms on six cards and initial consonants, consonant clusters, and consonant digraphs on 12 cards. Make a duplicate set of the cards. Place each set of cards in a resealable plastic bag. Place the cards, paper, pencils, and a sand timer in the shoe box. To play, have each child take a set of cards. Have children turn over the timer and move the cards around to build as many words as they can. They may reuse letters and word endings. When the time runs out, children check their lists for rhyming words. Players score one point for each word that has no rhymes on the list. They score two points for each word that has at least one rhyme on the list. Children can play again and try to beat their own scores.

We're Going on a Word Hunt!

Children practice ending sounds and spelling patterns as they hunt for objects in the classroom.

Stock a shoe box with small notepads, "detective" props (such as magnifying glasses), and pencils. Place a label on each notepad cover and write a phonogram group on it (such as "short-*a* phonograms"). Label sets of pages in each notepad with specific phonograms, such as *-ab*, *-ack*, *-act*, *-aft*, *-ag*, and *-am*. Have children select a notepad and, in a designated area of the classroom, search for examples of items with names that contain the word families and use words or pictures to record them. For example, a child with a short *a* notepad might notice and record *hat* (in a cubby), *mat* (on the floor), and *cat* (in a picture book) for the *-at* family.